Families Today

Building
Academic Skills

Glencoe
McGraw-Hill

New York, New York   Columbus, Ohio   Woodland Hills, California   Peoria, Illinois

Contributing Writer:
Janice P. Meek, CFCS

Glencoe/McGraw-Hill

*A Division of The **McGraw·Hill** Companies*

Printed in the United States of America

Send all inquiries to:
Glencoe/McGraw-Hill
3008 W. Willow Knolls Drive
Peoria, IL 61614

ISBN 0-07-820710-X

1 2 3 4 5 6 7 8 9 10 047 04 03 02 01 00 99

TABLE OF CONTENTS

Activity Title	Academic Skill	Page

Unit 1: The Family Foundation

Activity Title	Academic Skill	Page
Fran Tarkenton: A Look at Values	Language Arts	5
Democracy and Family	Social Studies	7
What's New?	Science	8
A Long and Happy Life	Health	9
Slice the Family Pie	Mathematics	10

Unit 2: Strengthening Relationships

Activity Title	Academic Skill	Page
The True Story	Language Arts	11
A House Divided	Social Studies	12
Relationships	Science	13
Family Wellness	Health	14
Family Vacations	Mathematics	15

Unit 3: Managing with Insight

Activity Title	Academic Skill	Page
Is It Really *Cheaper by the Dozen?*	Language Arts	16
His and Her Expectations	Social Studies	19
The Other Half of the Story	Science	20
The Best of Care	Health	23
Out to Eat?	Mathematics	24

Unit 4: Supporting Family and Friends

Activity Title	Academic Skill	Page
The Painful Side of Divorce	Language Arts	25
Leaders	Social Studies	28
Freud — After a Loved One Dies	Science	29
No Easy Answer	Health	31
Drugs and Crime	Mathematics	32

Unit 5: Extending Your Relationships

Activity Title	Academic Skill	Page
Speaking of Seniors	Language Arts	33
A Personal Bill of Rights	Social Studies	34
Magnetic Personalities	Science	35
Prescription for Elders	Health	36
Dates and Dollars	Mathematics	37

Unit 6: Growing as a Person

Activity Title	Academic Skill	Page
Pulling Strings	Language Arts	38
Givers and Takers	Social Studies	39
A Person of Vision	Social Studies	40
The Strength to Resist	Science	42
An Oath for Working	Health	44
What Shape Fits You?	Mathematics	45

Activity Title	Academic Skill	Page

Unit 7: Moving Toward Independence

A Toast for Every Occasion	Language Arts	46
Poor Richard's Advice	Social Studies	47
The Mother of Invention	Science	48
Rewards Offered!	Health	49
Favorite Brands	Mathematics	50

Unit 8: Forming Your Own Family

Bedtime	Language Arts	51
First Ladies	Social Studies	53
Using the Scientific Method	Science	55
Family Health Risks	Health	56
For Richer or Poorer	Mathematics	57
Answer Key		58

Building Academic Skills . . .

. . . contains activities that focus on language arts, social studies, science, health, and mathematics skills. At least one activity for each academic skill is provided for use with each of the eight units in the **Families Today** text. An Answer Key is provided at the end of the booklet.

◇ **Unit 1**
◇ **The Family Foundation**

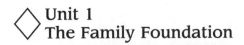

Building Academic Skills
Language Arts

FRAN TARKENTON: A LOOK AT VALUES

Directions: Attitudes and actions are a reflection of the values a person has. Many values are formed as the result of family influence. Read the following passage from the biography of Fran Tarkenton (*Fran Tarkenton — Scrambling Quarterback* by Julian May, Crestwood House, Inc., Mankato, Minnesota, 1977). Then answer the questions that follow.

He was a minister's boy.

For his first ten years he was small for his age. He had asthma, which sometimes made it hard for him to breathe. But that didn't stop him from playing on a boys' club football team in his home city of Washington, D.C.

When he wasn't on the field, he was in his bedroom, planning make-believe games. His team was the 1950 Philadelphia Eagles — on bubble-gum cards.

And he, Francis Tarkenton, was always the quarterback.

"Someday," he told himself, "I'll play quarterback in Yankee Stadium in New York. The whole world will cheer."

The Tarkenton family was very religious. But Fran's father did not worry about his son's interest in sports.

"God inspired me to become a pastor," he said to his son. "He may inspire you to become an athlete."

"I hope so!" said young Fran.

The family moved to Athens, Georgia, the next year. There were many good sports opportunities for boys. Fran began to grow tall and strong. He played football and basketball, and he was a star Little League Baseball pitcher. In 1952, Fran helped his Little League team win the city championship.

He entered Athens High the next year and was a good student. Sports were still the center of his life, however. Even as a freshman, he made the varsity teams in football, baseball, and basketball.

He liked baseball best. In 1954, he hit .365 and helped bring the team to the regional championships. There he struck out 26 men in 22 innings and batted .417. The team won the title after Fran pitched a one-hitter.

That fall, he went out for football again. As a frosh quarterback, he had spent most of his time studying the game. Now he was ready to win. Athens High took nine games out of ten that year. Then they met Rockmart for the playoff that would decide the North Georgia title.

With Fran Tarkenton as quarterback, the Athens squad dominated the game. The score was tied, 6-6, in the last minutes. According to the rules, Athens was about to be declared the winner on a technicality.

But this wasn't good enough for Fran. He decided to gamble on his team's ability to score again. He called a rollout pass to the right and threw.

The ball was intercepted. A Rockmart player ran away with it for a touchdown.

(Continued on next page)

Fran's gamble had lost his team the regional title. Some of the boys wept in the locker room. But Fran said, "We'll whip 'em next time."

Fran's first love was still baseball. He dreamed of becoming a major league pitcher. During the 1955 season, the Athens team was doing well and Fran was the star hurler.

Then they met Covington, a tough team to beat. Fran, standing out on the mound, studied the heavy hitter who was next up to bat. He thought, "I'll give the ball a little extra spin this time."

He wound up and threw. There was a sudden snap! The pitch went wild and Fran's arm exploded in pain. He had torn a tendon below the elbow. When it healed, he found that his pitching ability was gone forever. Much later, Fran would consider the accident a lucky one. It turned his attention from baseball to football, because strangely enough, he could throw a pass as well as ever.

Analyzing the Passage

1. Identify three values that you feel Fran showed. Describe what Fran did or said to show these values.

    a. _____

    _____

    _____

    b. _____

    _____

    _____

    c. _____

    _____

    _____

2. How do you think Fran's family may have influenced his values?

    _____

    _____

    _____

    _____

    _____

    _____

FAMILIES TODAY Building Academic Skills

◇ **Unit 1**
  The Family Foundation

DEMOCRACY AND FAMILY

Directions: James Daugherty was a well-known American painter and writer. As a young student at the London School of Art, Daugherty was inspired by the writings of Walt Whitman and his visions of America. In the book *Walt Whitman's America* (The World Publishing Co., Cleveland, Ohio, 1964), Daugherty compiled favorite Whitman selections with his own original illustrations as a tribute to Whitman's influence. One selection from Whitman's *Democratic Vistas* draws a vivid comparison between democracy and family. Read the passage and then answer the questions.

> DEMOCRACY . . . ALONE CAN BIND, and never seeks to bind, all nations, all men, of however various and distant lands, into a brotherhood, a family. It is the old, yet ever-modern dream of earth, out of her eldest and her youngest, her fond philosophers and poets. Not that half (of democracy) only, individualism, which isolates. There is another half, which is adhesiveness or love, that fuses, ties, and aggregates, making the races comrades, and fraternizing all.

1. According to Whitman, how is democracy like a family? _____

_____

2. Describe the two halves of democracy. _____

_____

_____

Do these two halves apply to the family as well? Explain your answer. _____

_____

3. Consult a dictionary to find definitions of *family* and *democracy*. Write the definitions in the space below.

Family: _____

Democracy: _____

What do the two definitions have in common? _____

_____

How do they differ? _____

_____

◇ **Unit 1**
The Family Foundation

WHAT'S NEW?

The twentieth century was a time of rapid change. New inventions, discoveries, and developments changed the way people lived, worked, and played. In 1900, most people used horses for transportation, candles and kerosene or oil lamps for lighting, and coal- or wood-burning stoves for cooking. The telephone had been invented but was not in wide use, and the Wright brothers' first flight was three years in the future. Many people, especially in rural areas, had no indoor plumbing.

Directions: On the chart below, list at least one effect each invention or discovery has had on society, families, or individuals. Then on the lines below the chart, describe the changes you think the twenty-first century will bring to that area.

Invention or Discovery	Effect
Air conditioning	
Computer	
Fax machine	
Polio vaccine	
Teflon	
Television	

_____

_____

_____

_____

_____

_____

_____

_____

◇ **Unit 1**
◇ **The Family Foundation**

A Long and Happy Life

Most people hope for a long and happy life. Life expectancy data show the likelihood of long life. Quality of life is a measure of how satisfying or happy life is.

Since 1900, the average life expectancy has increased from 47 to 76 years. The major causes of death in 1900 were contagious diseases — pneumonia, tuberculosis, and diseases of the stomach and intestines. Today's leading causes of death are heart disease, cancer, and stroke. None of these is contagious. Each of these diseases is greatly influenced by a person's way of living and his or her health habits.

Directions: Think about ways that increased life spans can affect the quality of life for individuals and families. Use the space below to write about these effects. If you wish, cite examples from the lives of people you know.

◇ **Unit 1**
The Family Foundation

SLICE THE FAMILY PIE

Directions: Survey your class to determine the number of students who live in each type of family listed below. Record your results in the "number" column.

Type of Family	Number	Percentage
Nuclear		
Single-parent		
Blended		
Extended		
Adoptive		
Foster		

Determine what percentage of the total is represented by each type of family. Record percentages in the last column. Then use the circle below to draw a pie chart representing your survey results. How does your classroom compare to what you know about national trends?

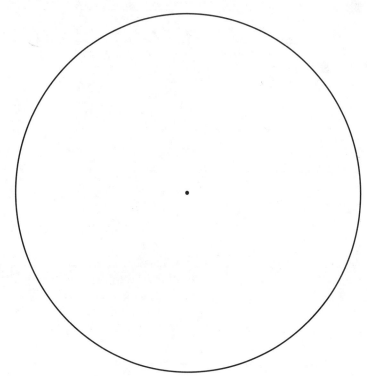

FAMILIES TODAY Building Academic Skills
Copyright © Glencoe/McGraw-Hill

◇ Unit 2
◇ Strengthening Relationships

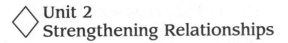

THE TRUE STORY

Characters on television are shown in a variety of relationship situations. Characters illustrate both good and bad communication skills. They show both constructive and destructive forms of conflict. Whether any of these glimpses of life are realistic or not is up to you as a viewer to decide.

Directions: Imagine that you are a writer and that you have been asked to create a new television show that depicts family life as it really is in the United States today. Write the title for your new television show below. Then describe the characters and setting, and give an outline of the story.

Title:

Characters:

Setting:

Story line:

◇ **Unit 2**
◇ **Strengthening Relationships**

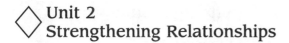

Building Academic Skills
Social Studies

A HOUSE DIVIDED

Abraham Lincoln was a man of principle and a president who understood the power of the spoken word. He was a master of public speaking, as he demonstrated in the Douglas debates, in his inaugural address, and in his famous Gettysburg Address.

Perhaps the most characteristic trademark of Lincoln's speeches was his ability to target main points in a few well-chosen words. In his immortal speech at Gettysburg, he succinctly stated America's purpose as a nation:

Fourscore and seven years ago our fathers brought forth upon this continent, a new nation, conceived in liberty, and dedicated to the proposition that all men are created equal.

In the Douglas debates of 1858, Lincoln stated, "A house divided against itself cannot stand." He was referring to the nation's division over the issue of slavery.

Consider the matter of unity. It may be applied to families as well as nations. Think about issues that can cause division in families. Can differences of opinion cause families to break down? How can a family deal with differing opinions and remain strong as a family unit?

Directions: In the space below write a paragraph (of 50 words or less) to address answers to the questions above. You may use the title, "A House Divided," or create an original title. Apply Lincoln's style: be brief, concise, and to the point.

FAMILIES TODAY Building Academic Skills
Copyright © Glencoe/McGraw-Hill

◇ Unit 2
◇ Strengthening Relationships

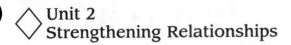

RELATIONSHIPS

Ecologists study relationships between organisms in a living community. Social scientists study relationships among family members and others in their environment. The disciplines of science and social science have a lot in common.

Directions: Read the following summary of relationships that exist in living communities. After reading, answer the question that follows.

All of the organisms in a given area make up the living community. These include animals, plants, microorganisms, and fungi.

Organisms may be producers, consumers, and/or decomposers. Producers are the organisms that produce food. Consumers are the organisms that get food from other organisms. Decomposers get their food from dead organisms or from wastes of organisms.

Organisms relate to each other in one of two ways. They have either a symbiotic or a competitive relationship.

Those organisms that depend on one another have symbiotic relationships. There are three forms of symbioses: parasites, mutualism, and commensalism. A parasite is an organism that feeds from another organism without killing it. In mutualism, two organisms derive benefits from each other. In a commensal relationship, one organism benefits, and the other is not affected.

Organisms that need the same things are said to be competitive. If the needed resources are limited, competition becomes very great. Usually, one of two things happens. Either one species will die out or be run out, or one will gradually change its needs in order for the two to coexist.

How does the discussion above relate to human relationships? Include specific examples to illustrate your response.

_____

_____

_____

_____

_____

_____

_____

◇ **Unit 2**
Strengthening Relationships

FAMILY WELLNESS

Directions: Many elements make up a healthy family climate. Most families have some things they do better than others. Read the list below, and look for those items that are strengths in your family. Place a check mark beside the three that you think your family does the best. Then follow the directions below the list.

Do family members . . .

_____ 1. Spend time together regularly?

_____ 2. Show respect for one another?

_____ 3. Face problems directly?

_____ 4. Discuss disagreements calmly?

_____ 5. Set family goals and work to reach them?

_____ 6. Avoid taking out stresses on one another?

_____ 7. Enjoy being together?

_____ 8. Assume their fair share of responsibility for household work?

_____ 9. Express love and concern for one another?

_____ 10. Have and follow family rules?

_____ 11. Try to understand one another's viewpoints?

_____ 12. Participate in family traditions?

_____ 13. Pull together when there is a serious problem?

_____ 14. Make commitment to family a high priority?

_____ 15. Talk to one another?

Choose two items from the list above that you think are most important to family wellness. Explain why you have selected these two.

a. _____

_____

_____

_____

b. _____

_____

_____

_____

◇ Unit 2
◇ Strengthening Relationships

Building Academic Skills
Math

FAMILY VACATIONS

Families have long enjoyed the chance to "get away from it all" by taking a family vacation. Certainly, vacations can help families spend quality time together, talk things over, and gain new perspectives. The main disadvantage of vacations for some families is the cost factor. Having a clear idea of vacation costs can help family members plan and save for such expenses.

Directions: Plan a five-day (four nights) vacation for four to the place of your choice. Use your research skills to complete the chart below, estimating what such a trip might cost in total.

Vacation Destination _____

Transportation
  Auto (total mileage): _____ × $ _____ /mile =   _____

  Air fare (round trip): _____ × 4 people =   _____

Lodging
  Type: _____ at $ _____ /night × 4 nights =   _____

Food
  Breakfast: _____ × 5 days =   _____

  Lunch: _____ × 5 days =   _____

  Dinner: _____ × 5 days =   _____

  Snacks: _____ × 5 days =   _____

Entertainment (includes admissions and souvenirs)

  _____ =   _____

  _____ =   _____

  _____ =   _____

  _____ =   _____

Estimated Total Cost of Trip   _____

◇ **Unit 3**
◇ **Managing with Insight**

IS IT REALLY *CHEAPER BY THE DOZEN?*

Directions: Read the following passage taken from the book *Cheaper by the Dozen* (Thomas Y. Crowell Co., 1948). This book was written by Frank B. Gilbreth, Jr., and Ernestine Gilbreth Carey, two of the children in a family of twelve children. The authors tell the story of their family life with Mother, Dad, and their brothers and sisters during the years 1910 to 1924. Mother and Dad were among the first professionals in the field of scientific management and were quite accomplished as efficiency experts. The book shows how management skills, combined with a keen sense of humor, make for a very positive family climate. As you read, ask yourself the question: Can it really be "cheaper by the dozen"? After reading the selection, answer the questions that follow.

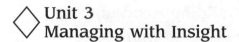

One reason he had so many children — there were twelve of us — was that he was convinced anything he and Mother teamed up on was sure to be a success.

Dad always practiced what he preached, and it was just about impossible to tell where his scientific management company ended and his family life began. His office was always full of children, and he often took two or three of us, and sometimes all twelve, on business trips. Frequently, we'd tag along at his side, pencils and notebooks in our hands, when Dad toured a factory which had hired him as an efficiency expert.

On the other hand, our house at Montclair, New Jersey, was sort of a school for scientific management and the elimination of wasted motions — or "motion study," as Dad and Mother named it.

Dad took moving pictures of us children washing dishes, so that he could figure out how we could reduce our motions and thus hurry through the task. Irregular jobs, such as painting the back porch or removing a stump from the front lawn, were awarded on a low-bid basis. Each child who wanted extra pocket money submitted a sealed bid saying what he would do the job for. The lowest bidder got the contract.

Dad installed process and work charts in the bathrooms. Every child old enough to write — and Dad expected his off-spring to start writing at a tender age — was required to initial the charts in the morning after he had brushed his teeth, taken a bath, combed his hair, and made his bed. At night, each child had to weigh himself, plot the figure on a graph, and initial process charts again after he had done his homework, washed his hands and face, and brushed his teeth. Mother wanted to have a place on the charts for saying prayers, but Dad said as far as he was concerned prayers were voluntary.

It was regimentation, all right. But bear in mind the trouble most parents have in getting just one child off to school, and multiply it by twelve. Some regimentation was necessary to prevent bedlam. Of course there were times when a child would initial the charts without actually having fulfilled the requirements. However, Dad had a gimlet eye and a terrible swift sword. The combined effect was that truth usually went marching on.

(Continued on next page)

FAMILIES TODAY Building Academic Skills
Copyright © Glencoe/McGraw-Hill

Yes, at home or on the job, Dad was always the efficiency expert. He buttoned his vest from the bottom up, instead of from the top down, because the bottom-to-top process took him only three seconds, while the top-to-bottom took seven. He even used two shaving brushes to lather his face, because he found that by doing so he could cut seventeen seconds off his shaving time. For a while he tried shaving with two razors, but he finally gave that up.

"I can save forty-four seconds," he grumbled, "but I wasted two minutes this morning putting this bandage on my throat."

It wasn't the slashed throat that really bothered him. It was the two minutes.

Some people used to say that Dad had so many children he couldn't keep track of them. Dad himself used to tell a story about one time when Mother went off to fill a lecture engagement and left him in charge at home. When Mother returned, she asked him if everything had run smoothly.

"Didn't have any trouble except with that one over there," he replied. "But a spanking brought him into line."

"That's not one of ours, dear," she said. "He belongs next door."

None of us remembers it, and maybe it never happened. Dad wasn't above stretching the truth, because there was nothing he liked better than a joke, particularly if it were on him and even more particularly if it were on Mother. This much is certain, though. There were two red-haired children who lived next door, and the Gilbreths all are blondes or red heads.

Analyzing the Passage

1. What is "motion economy"? Cite one or more examples of Dad Gilbreth's use of motion economy.

_____

_____

_____

2. Name two tasks that must be done in your family but could be made easier with motion economy.

_____

_____

3. What are process and work charts? List specific items Dad included on these.

_____

_____

_____

4. How might your family make use of a work chart?

_____

_____

(Continued on next page)

5. How did Dad prepare his children for their future roles in the work world?

_____

_____

_____

6. What family living experiences have you had that taught you something useful about working?

_____

_____

_____

_____

7. Why did Dad quit shaving with two razors?

_____

_____

8. How did Dad show a sense of humor?

_____

_____

9. How important is a sense of humor in a family? Explain your reasoning.

_____

_____

_____

10. Do you think that it really was "cheaper by the dozen" to manage as a family during the time period of 1910 to 1924? Why or why not? Do you think it would be cheaper today? Why or why not?

_____

_____

_____

_____

_____

FAMILIES TODAY Building Academic Skills

◇ Unit 3
◇ Managing with Insight

HIS AND HER EXPECTATIONS

Controversy over the role expectations of males and females continues to exist. Although times have changed, people still don't always agree on what is appropriate behavior for each gender.

Directions: Use the checklist below to explore your own thinking about role expectations by placing a check mark under "yes" or "no" for each question. Now, keep this checklist for your own reference while comparing your results with other class members. Discuss the reasoning behind attitudes, and identify any problems that might result from differing opinions.

Is it appropriate for . . .	Yes	No
1. Males to babysit?		
2. Females to ask males out?		
3. Males to cry?		
4. Females to play in contact sports?		
5. Males to become nurses?		
6. Females to aim for political office?		
7. Males to be house-husbands?		
8. Females to be major breadwinners?		
9. Females to have higher incomes than husbands?		
10. Males to play with dolls?		
11. Females to play with trucks?		
12. Males to enjoy home decorating?		
13. Females to enjoy building?		
14. Males to do needlework?		
15. Females to open doors for males?		
16. Males to give up their seat on a bus?		
17. Males to stand when females enter?		
18. Females to shake hands?		
19. Males to choose not to marry?		
20. Females to choose not to marry?		
21. Males to choose not to be fathers?		
22. Females to choose not to be mothers?		

◇ **Unit 3**
◇ **Managing with Insight**

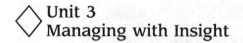

Building Academic Skills
Science

THE OTHER HALF OF THE STORY

Directions: Read the following passage condensed from "A Consumer's Guide to Environmental Myths and Realities." Then answer the questions that follow.

In recent years, numerous groups, including federal agencies, have offered counsel on how Americans can be "good environmentalists." Although well-intentioned, the advice is too often based on little more than uncritical acceptance of such core beliefs as "recycling is good." From the perspective of the total environment, the advice is frequently wrong. Those who follow it may actually end up harming the environment more than if they were to ignore it altogether.

Here are five common myths:

Packaging is bad

This idea is now widely accepted by consumers who are concerned about the environment. But it's not necessarily true. Packaging can actually prevent certain kinds of waste.

When a food is processed and packaged in the United States, byproducts such as rinds and peels are often used as fuel, animal feed, or in another economically useful way. By contrast, in Mexico, where packaging is less prevalent, such food byproducts become garbage. Compared with the United States, the average Mexican household throws away three times more food debris — 1.6 pounds per household per day, according to a University of Arizona study.

Food packaging also reduces spoilage. The complex layering of metal and plastics that helps keep some Keebler snacks fresh for up to six months, for example, lets the company distribute them throughout the country without having a plant in every city. Such packaging meets consumer needs and economizes on the use of resources.

Recycling is always good

In principle, most waste products — iron and steel, aluminum, glass, paper, and even tires — can be recycled. And, in fact, a great deal of recycling already takes place. More than 50 million tons of scrap iron and steel are recycled each year, as are 16 million tires. Over half of the aluminum cans in the United States are recycled, as well as one-fourth of the glass and plastic beverage containers.

But would universal recycling necessarily be better for the environment? The answer is no.

Recycling has environmental side effects. Curbside garbage-recycling programs often require more collection trucks — which means more fuel consumption and more air pollution. Some recycling programs use large amounts of energy and produce high volumes of water waste. Distant recycling facilities often necessitate considerable resources just to transport the stuff there.

Take paper recycling. Proponents argue that every ton of recycled newsprint saves 17 trees. But most of the trees used to make paper are planted explicitly for manufacturing paper. Less paper from virgin pulp means fewer trees planted by commercial harvesters. According to a study by Resources for the Future, a nonpartisan research organization in Washington, D.C., the net effect of universal paper recycling could actually be a decline in tree planting and tree coverage, as lands are converted to other uses.

(Continued on next page)

FAMILIES TODAY Building Academic Skills
Copyright © Glencoe/McGraw-Hill

Nonbiodegradable products are bad

Consumers have been told: anything that decomposes naturally is good, and anything that does not is bad. But most modern landfills are capped, inhibiting biodegradation of anything.

Biodegradable products, if disposed of improperly, can leach dangerous chemicals into the water supply. Nonbiodegradable products, for the most part, do not have this problem.

Disposables are bad

A 1990 children's television special produced by Home Box Office was designed to teach this idea. So, too, was the first version of the Environmental Protection Agency's booklet "The Environmental Consumer's Handbook." It was withdrawn after some members of the EPA's own staff complained about "oversimplification and inaccuracies."

Here are two examples of what's wrong. Some environmentalists have targeted juice boxes because they contribute to waste. But transporting empty glass bottles requires more trucks than transporting empty boxes, using more fuel and causing air pollution. And aseptic packages don't need refrigeration, saving energy.

Disposable diapers are also denounced as wasteful. But over its "lifetime," a cloth diaper uses six times more water than a disposable does. This matters a lot in western states, such as California, where landfill space is relatively abundant, but water is scarce. California residents who avoid disposables and wash cloth diapers may not be doing their environment a favor.

Plastics are bad

To most advocates of "green" consumerism, an aluminum container is best, glass second and plastic the worst. However, according to the economic and environmental research organization California Futures, of nonrecycled containers, plastic takes the least energy to manufacture.

Several municipalities have begun to ban some kinds of plastic goods on the assumption that plastics contribute to our waste problem. Actually, plastic materials comprise only about eight percent of municipal solid waste by weight.

Plastics are lighter and more efficient than many other kinds of packaging. A research organization in Germany examined the effects of eliminating all plastic packaging in that country. It found that energy consumption would almost double and the weight of solid wastes would increase 404 percent.

There's no doubt that Americans throw away a lot of stuff — about 180 million tons of solid waste annually. But the amount of waste discarded into landfills has remained fairly constant for decades. As William Rathje, a leading expert on garbage, has observed: "Americans are wasteful, but we have been conditioned to think of ourselves as more wasteful than we truly are." While we seek to protect the environment, let us take care to look beyond the "simple" rules that may do more harm than good.

Condensed from "A Consumer's Guide to Environmental Myths and Realities" by Lynn Scarlett, The National Center for Policy Analysis, Dallas, Texas 75243
Reader's Digest, May, 1992
Pleasantville, N.Y. 10570

(Continued on next page)

For Analysis

1. For eachm of the myths listed, name a reality cited by the author of the article.

   Packaging is bad: _____

   _____

   Recycling is always good: _____

   _____

   Nonbiodegradable products are bad: _____

   _____

   Disposables are bad: _____

   _____

   Plastics are bad: _____

   _____

2. Would a study on packaging likely be more reliable if done by a food manufacturer or an independent research organization? Explain your reasoning.

   _____

   _____

   _____

3. People often say that there are two sides to every story. How does this relate to the article?

   _____

   _____

   _____

4. Does this article promote the idea that environmental concerns are not worth pursuing? Explain your answer.

   _____

   _____

   _____

   _____

FAMILIES TODAY Building Academic Skills
Copyright © Glencoe/McGraw-Hill

◇ **Unit 3**
◇ **Managing with Insight**

THE BEST OF CARE

Directions: Getting health care today often means choosing the right specialist. Listed below are some of the basic types of medical specialists needed at one time or another by family members. Use a dictionary or health resource to describe below what type of care each one provides.

Medical Specialists	Care Provided
Allergist	
Audiologist	
Cardiologist	
Dental Hygienist	
Dentist	
Dermatologist	
Emergency Medical Technician	
Gastroenterologist	
Geriatric Physician	
Gynecologist	
Neurologist	
Obstetrician	
Oncologist	
Ophthalmologist	
Orthopedist	
Pediatrician	
Pharmacist	
Physical Therapist	
Podiatrist	
Psychiatrist	
Psychologist	
Respiratory Therapist	
Urologist	

Name _____ Date _____ Class Period _____

◇ Unit 3
Managing with Insight

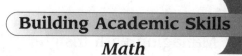

OUT TO EAT?

Directions: Today's fast-paced lifestyles have made eating out a regular routine for many, but doing so may result in poor nutrition. It may also have a negative impact on the budget. Try comparing the costs of eating out and in. First, fill in one of your favorite menus (one to three items). Then, call or visit three restaurants to obtain prices for the items on the menu. Finally, list the ingredients needed to prepare the meal at home, and visit a grocery store to get prices. Which is more economical in this case, out or in?

The menu is: _____

Restaurant	Menu Item	Price
Total:		
Total:		
Total:		

Ingredients for Each Menu Item	Cost	Cost Per Serving
Item:		
Item:		
Item:		
Total Cost of Preparing Menu	

24

FAMILIES TODAY Building Academic Skills
Copyright © Glencoe/McGraw-Hill

◇ **Unit 4**
◇ **Supporting Family and Friends**

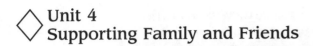

Building Academic Skills
Language Arts

THE PAINFUL SIDE OF DIVORCE

Directions: Divorce brings trauma to even the most solid family unit. Read the following excerpt about one young man's reaction to divorce from the novel *Necessary Parties* by Barbara Dana (Harper & Row, Publishers, New York, 1986). Then discuss the questions that follow with your class. (To find out how Chris tackled and solved his problem of family breakdown, read further in the novel.)

My father folded his napkin in consecutive geometric layers and set it under the side of his plate. "Your mother and I are getting a divorce."

It was like my whole insides gave way. There was this sense of falling. I wanted to grab on to something, but everything was evaporating and there was nothing there. Then the phone rang.

Oh, God, I thought, not the phone. Isn't the news enough, the announcement of the end of our world? Isn't that enough to bear without having to deal with a person on the phone? Somebody should answer it, I thought, but I couldn't move.

My father just went on. "I know you understand what this means, Chris, so I'm going to address myself to Jenny, but everything I say goes for you, too."

The phone rang again.

"The phone's ringing," said Jenny.

"I know," said Dad. "For a long time now Mommy and I haven't been getting along very well. There have been a lot of fights. Have you noticed that?"

"Bunny has."

"Bunny has. Yes, well, right. He's right. There have been a lot of fights. Too many, and that's not good."

The phone rang again. My dad got up to answer it. My mother kept staring at the tablecloth. I could hear my dad on the phone — business. "Tell him it's now or never," he was saying. "We can't wait around."

I started feeling dizzy.

"Can I call you back in ten minutes?"

TEN MINUTES? Our lives are at stake and he gives it TEN MINUTES?

Dad hung up the phone and returned to the table. Jenny was removing the tape that attached Funny Bunny Richardson to the stool. "Bunny's leaving," she said.

"Let Daddy finish," said my dad. "Sit down now and don't fiddle with the tape."

Jenny sat down. Then my dad went into his speech about divorce and what it means. I swear (and I don't do that often) but I swear it was the stupidest and most nonsensical speech I had ever heard. It was like I was in the midst of a black comedy, some bizarre, unwanted satire on the reasonableness of the insane. I wanted to scream, but I felt somehow paralyzed.

"Now, as I said earlier," my dad continued, "we love you both very much and that will never change. But sometimes the person you marry changes and sometimes you change."

Don't say "change" again, I remember thinking. I felt that if he said "change" one more time I would go for his throat.

(Continued on next page)

"Mommy and I have both changed in the sixteen years since we've been married."

There it is, I thought. He said it. The past tense does not get him off the hook.

"We don't make each other happy anymore, so we have to make a change. And that change will be a divorce."

Why? Aren't there other kinds of changes? Can't people change for the better, bring out the best in each other?

"We're going to be getting a divorce and what that means, Jenny, is that we won't be living in the same house anymore. You and I will be living in the same house sometimes, and you and Mommy will be living in the same house sometimes, but Mommy and I will be living in different houses."

He was trying to make it sound like a nice idea, but it wasn't working. I felt this wave of total lack of respect for him, which scared the hell out of me. This was my dad who I loved and who had taught me so much and taken care of me and been my friend and ordered presents for me from Eddie Bauer in the middle of the night and held my hand when I had nightmares from the measles.

My mother reached out her arms to Jenny. "Come here, sweetheart," she said.

Jenny got off her chair and climbed into my mom's lap. She curled into a kind of ball.

My dad kept going. "So, Jenny, you and Chris will live with Mommy part of the time and with me part of the time, the time you're not living with Mommy. But Mommy and I won't be living in the same house, not anymore. Mommy will stay in this house, for a while at least, and I will have an apartment in the city, so when you live with me you'll be in the city and when you live with Mommy you'll be here, for a while, at least."

The room started to spin and I felt I was either going to pass out or throw up. My mother was stroking Jenny's hair. Then the phone rang and I totally freaked out.

"NO!" I screamed. I jumped up and ran to the phone, ready to rip it out of the wall.

Coward, I thought.

I simply lifted the receiver. "WE CAN'T TALK NOW!" I shouted into the phone. Then I slammed the phone down and turned to my dad.

"YOU CAN'T DO THIS!"

"You're upset," he said. "Let's talk about it."

"I DON'T WANT TO TALK ABOUT IT!"

"Please, Chris," said my mother.

"YOU'RE NOT GOING TO DO THIS!"

"It's not up to you, Chris," said my dad.

The phone rang and I turned and left the house. I slammed the front door and found myself in the front yard in the dark. I had to pace, to move. I started wildly circling the large oak tree, ready to pull it out by its roots. Now who was going crazy? Inside I could see Mom was holding Jenny, and my dad on the phone. That was almost the worst part of the whole thing to me, at that moment anyway. How could he be on the phone at a time like this? I kept circling the tree, then pacing back and forth, the energy building and building inside of me.

WHERE IS MY FAMILY?

Just then I spotted our Halloween pumpkins on the front steps, Jenny's and mine, a gift to the children of Bedford from the Bixler Real Estate Company. They had grotesque and jagged smiles (the pumpkins, not the Bixler Real Estate Company), and were rotting, with dark patches and green mold beginning to grow. I felt this immense hatred for those pumpkins. They took on a whole new meaning for me, the fact that they would rot and turn ugly like that.

(Continued on next page)

FAMILIES TODAY Building Academic Skills
Copyright © Glencoe/McGraw-Hill

Everything rots, I thought. Everything changes. WHY?

The pumpkins symbolized my family to me. I grabbed my leaving Jenny's to rot in peace, and carried it to the back house. It was truly disintegrating. My fingers went into layers soft mush and green, slimy fur. I had to destroy the pumpkin stamp out the rot (The Demise of the Bixler Pumpkin). Somewhere there was a twisted logic to it, but how it would help my family I'm not sure. Behind our house is a bird sanctuary. It's down a hill, forty acres of woods. I ran toward the hill and the woods and hurled the pumpkin over the side. It hit some rocks and truly exploded. A cat-aclysmic array of exploding pumpkin. I stood there, breathing heavily for a few minutes, and then just sat down on the grass and cried.

I wish I had a dog, I thought. I could hold on to him and cry. You can't hold on to fish.

For Discussion

1. Describe the reaction of each family member (Chris, Jenny, Mom, and Dad) to the divorce decision. What emotions do you think each is feeling?

2. What are some of the most difficult changes for family members as they deal with divorce?

3. Explain the significance of the Halloween pumpkins to Chris.

4. When it comes to families, do you agree with Chris when he says "Everything rots"? Why or why not?

◇ Unit 4
◇ Supporting Family and Friends

LEADERS

The challenge of change in the world would never be met without leaders. Leaders are those who make a difference. Leaders are change agents. They see a need, set strategies for change, and see them through.

The history books are filled with accounts of leaders who made a difference in the nation and world. They are the presidents, the prime ministers, and the popes. They are the scholars and scientists who have led the quest for knowledge. They are the common people as well, without title or degree, whose actions set them apart as leaders.

Directions: What extraordinary qualities do leaders possess? What approaches are used by successful leaders? To find out, select a leader, past or present, in whom you are interested. Research his or her life and work. Complete the outline below to summarize your findings. Share results with classmates.

The Leader: _____

Accomplishments: _____

_____

_____

_____

_____

Extraordinary Traits: _____

_____

_____

_____

_____

Approaches Used as a Leader: _____

_____

_____

_____

_____

◇ **Unit 4**
◇ **Supporting Family and Friends**

FREUD — AFTER A LOVED ONE DIES

Sigmund Freud is known as the father of psychoanalysis. His theories revolutionized the field of medicine and led the way to new understanding of human behavior. Freud considered areas that had never before been viewed as significant. He explored dreams, hidden memories, and subconscious feelings. During the time following the death of his father, Freud experienced firsthand some of the reactions he had seen in his own patients.

Directions: Read the following passage from *Explorer of the Unconscious: Sigmund Freud,* a biography by Adrien Stoutenburg and Laura Nelson Baker (Charles Scribner's Sons, New York, 1965). Then discuss the questions that follow with your class.

The summer following his father's death marked a turning point in Freud's life. He, who in later years would be noted for a deep serenity of spirit, was in 1897 going through what he himself called a kind of neurotic experience which threatened to bring him to a complete breakdown. At times he felt totally unable to work but would wander restlessly from one distraction to another, playing chess or cards or mechanically studying ancient maps. Martha, for all her love and attention to every practical detail that would give him comfort, watched helplessly.

Freud's physical health plagued him also. His old enemy, migraine headache, afflicted him regularly, and he had long been a sufferer from nasal catarrh and sinus trouble. Twice, Fliess operated on him to drain off pus collected in the antrums, hollow spaces in the bone above the nose. Financial pressures, too, remained a problem. Aside from the expenses for his own family, he had to contribute to the support of his mother and his two remaining unmarried sisters, Adolfine and Paula. Anna and Eli had emigrated to America. Alexander was doing well in his transportation management work, but though he helped out with the expenses of their sisters and mother, he was not rich.

All these pressures (including challenges to his own theories), in addition to his strong reaction to his father's death and a beginning of conflict in his friendship with Fliess, worked to make him face the need to begin an intense self-analysis. This he started in July, 1897, combining it with his study of dreams, especially his own dreams.

"I believe I am in a cocoon," he wrote to Fliess, "and God knows what kind of beast will creep out of it."

In attempting to psychoanalyze himself, Freud was as much a pioneer as all who set off to travel uncharted paths have been. He had no guide except his own mind and intuition, no resources except his courage and unsparing self-honesty. It was an overwhelmingly lonely form of exploration, this going down into the labyrinth of oneself. During the process he began to experience all the things that as a third party he had witnessed going on in his patients, days when he went about depressed because he had understood nothing of the day's dreams, fantasies or mood. Then there were days when, like a flash of lightening, understanding would come and the dark corners would be revealed.

(Continued on next page)

Back home in Vienna in October, Freud pressed ahead with self-analysis and the study of dreams, his pen busily covering pages of manuscript paper as he recorded theory and experience in the clear, readable style that is typical of all his writings. When not writing, he might sit brooding, looking at the large collection of figurines and primitive sculpture that took up more and more space in his study. The year before he had made a trip to Bologna and Ravenna with Alexander and, finally, to Florence. Freud fell in love with Italy, especially the Galileo Museum near Florence with its ancient cultural treasures. Now examples of Florentine statuary were among his treasures. Often while sitting listening to a patient, he would take a figurine or paperweight or other object from his collection and sit turning it over and over in his hands as if the handling of some physical object increased the pitch of his mental concentration. He did the same thing now, while burrowing into his own mind and memories.

He had become convinced that the first years of an individual's life had a profound effect on his personality and character. Experiences entirely forgotten by the conscious part of the mind remained in the unconscious as in a dimly lighted storehouse, affecting action and thought. Only by probing that dimness with a strong searchlight could one hope to see through the springs of individual behavior. Dream study and psychoanalysis, he believed, were the twin searchlights to reveal the past and thereby perhaps cure psychoneuroses.

One of his own dreams particularly interested him: a dream of a man with one eye, short, fat and high-shouldered, who seemed to be a doctor. Reflecting on the dream later, he had decided the dream figure must represent a one-eyed professor he had once had. However, he had liked the professor, but he had felt a distinct dislike for the one-eyed man in his dream.

On his Sunday call at his mother's he asked her to describe the doctor who had delivered him when he had been born. Amalie readily recalled that the doctor had been one-eyed and, in fact, matched every other characteristic in Freud's dream.

But why the dislike for the dream doctor then? Freud mused. Surely he didn't resent the man's help in bringing him into the world.

"He's the same doctor," his mother added, "who treated you when you fell from a stool and cut open your jaw on the table."

Freud touched the spot where his beard covered the scar. Consciously he remembered nothing of the accident which had happened when he was three, but obviously his unconscious did and had associated the pain of the event with the one-eyed doctor, thus creating the dream feeling of resentment.

Reprinted by permission of Curtis Brown, Ltd.

For Discussion

1. Give examples of the stages of grief experienced by Freud after the death of his father.

2. How did his wife, Martha, offer her love and support during Freud's time of grief?

3. Why did Freud begin an intense self-analysis?

4. Is it possible that Freud's feelings about his father's death could have affected him for as much as a year? Explain your answer.

◇ Unit 4
◇ Supporting Family and Friends

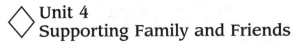

Building Academic Skills
Health

NO EASY ANSWER

Changes in medical technology and care have brought to the forefront some questions that are not easy to answer. One deals with the efforts that are made to keep people alive when death is near.

Modern medicine now has the means to prolong life, even in cases where there is little or no hope for recovery. Some people prefer to die naturally rather than hang on in pain or without awareness of what's going on. Some have written living wills to let their closest relatives know their wishes, requesting that no extraordinary measures be taken to prolong their life. There are, of course, two sides to this issue.

Directions: Use the space below to list possible reasons for taking measures to prolong a life. Next, list reasons for letting death occur naturally. Then answer the question at the bottom of the page.

Reasons for Prolonging Life	Reasons for Allowing Natural Death

Who do you think should be responsible for deciding whether to take extraordinary measures to prolong a life? Why?

_____

_____

_____

_____

◇ **Unit 4**
Supporting Family and Friends

DRUGS AND CRIME

Directions: Study the table below and answer the questions that follow. Note that although alcohol is a drug, it is categorized separately in this chart. What conclusions can you draw from this chart?

Violent offenders under the influence of drugs or alcohol, as perceived by victims									Note: Percents may not total 100% because of rounding. *Estimate is based on 10 or fewer sample cases. Source: *Criminal Victimization in the United States, 1989.*
Percent of violent crime victimizations where victim perceived the offender to be:				Under the influence					
Type of crime	Total	Not under the influence	Total	Alcohol only	Drugs only	Both	Not sure which substance	Not known if under the influence	
Crimes of violence	100%	18.1%	36.0%	21.0%	7.6%	5.6%	1.8%	45.9%	
Rape	100	10.6*	37.4	21.2	7.2*	9.0*	0*	52.0	
Robbery	100	12.2	27.4	8.9	12.2	4.5	1.8	60.4	
Aggravated assault	100	13.0	41.2	23.4	9.6	6.4	1.8	45.9	
Simple assault	100	23.5	36.2	24.0	4.8	5.3	1.9	40.4	

"Drugs and Crime Facts," 1991, United States Department of Justice

Using the Table

_____ 1. As reported by crime victims, what percentage of rape offenders were believed to be under the influence of alcohol only?

_____ 2. As reported by crime victims, in what type of crime were the largest percentage of offenders believed to be under the influence of drugs other than alcohol?

_____ 3. As reported by crime victims, what type of crime had the largest percentage of offenders who were believed to be under the influence of both alcohol and other drugs at the same time?

_____ 4. As reported by victims, in crimes of violence what percentage of offenders were believed to be under the influence of alcohol or other drugs, but the victim was not sure which?

_____ 5. In crimes of simple assault, what is the total percentage of offenders who were believed to be under the influence of alcohol, other drugs, or both?

_____ 6. In crimes of simple assault, what percentage of offenders were believed to be *not* under the influence of alcohol and/or other drugs?

_____ 7. In crimes of simple assault, what percentage of offenders were not known if under the influence of alcohol and/or other drugs?

_____ 8. What is the total of the answers to questions 5, 6, and 7? Does this answer reflect an error in the chart? Explain.

FAMILIES TODAY Building Academic Skills
Copyright © Glencoe/McGraw-Hill

◇ Unit 5
◇ Extending Your Relationships

SPEAKING OF SENIORS

Senior adults are often stereotyped inaccurately and unfairly. They are often thought of as sickly, set in their ways, and absentminded. While some seniors may fit stereotyped images, many do not. In order to form an impression of seniors, you need to spend time with them as individuals. Giving them an opportunity to state their feelings and opinions can help you see them as they really are.

Directions: Plan to interview a senior adult. Use the following space to write interview questions that will help you form an accurate impression. Conduct the interview. Record answers. Be prepared to share your findings and impressions with others in the class.

INTERVIEW QUESTIONS
1.
2.
3.
4.
5.
6.
7.
8.
9.
10.

◇ Unit 5
◇ Extending Your Relationships

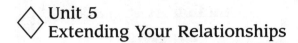

Building Academic Skills
Scoial Studies

A PERSONAL BILL OF RIGHTS

As a citizen of the United States of America, you are guaranteed certain basic rights. The first ten amendments to the United States Constitution are known as the Bill of Rights. These amendments name specific rights and guarantees to which all citizens are entitled. The first amendment, for example, says that you have the right to freedom of religion, speech, press, assembly, and petition.

Directions: Every person should have certain rights associated with being part of relationships outside the family. What should these rights be? Formulate ten personal rights and list them in the space below. Consider what responsibilities should accompany each right.

Personal Bill of Rights

1. _____

2. _____

3. _____

4. _____

5. _____

6. _____

7. _____

8. _____

9. _____

10. _____

FAMILIES TODAY Building Academic Skills

◇ **Unit 5**
◇ **Extending Your Relationships**

MAGNETIC PERSONALITIES

Directions: Read the following passage and answer the questions that follow.

Extending relationships means reaching out to people beyond your family, perhaps to those in your school and community. People who have "magnetic personalities" tend to attract others easily. Some people, however, find it takes a lot of effort to break out of their shells and reach out to new relationships.

In the field of science another kind of magnetism exists. Think about the principles of magnetism and see if you can do some comparing to what happens with people.

Some magnets occur naturally; others are made. Magnetite, for example, has the natural ability to attract iron. Artificial magnets are made from magnetic materials. Every magnet has two poles, north and south. On a bar magnet, the two ends are the poles. The power of the magnet is concentrated in the regions near each of these ends. If a magnet is cut into two pieces, two magnets are produced, both with north and south poles. When a north pole and a south pole are placed together, they pull together. Two north poles or two south poles placed together, however, will push away from each other. In other words, opposites attract and likes repel. Some magnets have a stronger force than others. Some keep their magnetism longer than others. The power of magnetism has long held the interest of people.

Making Comparisons

1. Does the "magnetic personality" of some people occur naturally or is it made? Explain your reasoning.

   _____

   _____

2. Do you think that the "opposites attract" principle applies to people as well as to magnets? Explain your answer.

   _____

   _____

3. Do some people have more "magnetism" than others? Why? _____

   _____

   _____

4. What traits do you believe comprise a "magnetic personality"? _____

   _____

   _____

◇ **Unit 5**
Extending Your Relationships

PRESCRIPTION FOR ELDERS

Elders may undergo physical and other types of changes, but they still have the same basic human needs as people of other ages. According to Abraham Maslow, these needs are best understood when arranged in a pyramid format. The pyramid shows basic physical needs at the bottom as the most urgent or basic group of needs. When these needs are not met, other needs that are higher on the pyramid become a lesser priority. Above physical needs are those of safety and security, love and belonging, esteem, and self-actualization, in ascending order. Self-actualization means reaching your fullest potential as an individual.

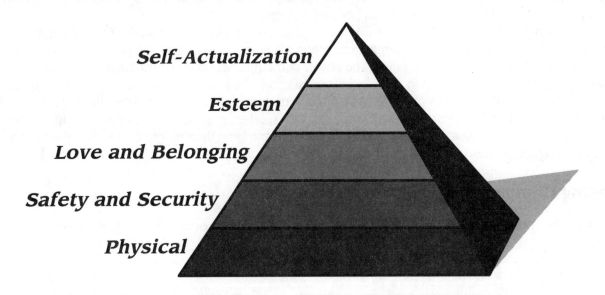

Directions: Think of an elderly person you know. Use the space below to list the needs you believe this person has. Then write a "prescription" for meeting one of the needs.

Needs: _____

_____

_____

Prescription: _____

_____

_____

_____

◇ **Unit 5**
◇ **Extending Your Relationships**

DATES AND DOLLARS

Dating is a great way to get to know people and to have fun at the same time. Dating presents many opportunities for decision-making — whom to date, when to go out, and where to go — just to name a few. The costs of dating must be a factor in dating decisions as well.

Who pays the expenses on a date? The answer depends on the person you ask. Young people's expectations for male and female dating roles depend largely on their family, community, and ethnic background. Some males are happy to have the female pay half of the expenses. Other people may think that it is the male's role to pay all expenses. The important thing to remember is that both the male and female should be sensitive to the other's views. They should not assume that their views are the same.

Directions: Regardless of who is paying, costs should be considered by both parties. Fill in the blanks below to get a clearer picture of what a date might cost. Then in the box, plan one date that you would enjoy, itemizing the costs involved and computing the total cost.

What do these typically cost for two people on a date?

Meal _____

Snacks _____

Skating _____

Dance _____

Movie _____

Ballgame _____

Bowling _____

Transportation _____

Costs for One Date

Plan: _____

_____

Costs:

_____ _____

_____ _____

_____ _____

_____ _____

_____ _____

Total _____

◇ Unit 6
◇ Growing as a Person

PULLING STRINGS

Have you ever noticed how much other people affect your moods? You may start the day feeling positive and optimistic. Then you run into a friend who talks on and on about problems and complaints until your good mood vanishes. On the other hand, you may be feeling tired and short-tempered until a friend's joke or a stranger's unexpected kindness helps you see the bright side again. If you think about it, you will realize that other people have a strong influence on you. They affect your moods and your self-concept. Even when you are unaware, other people may be "pulling your strings."

Directions: Develop an idea for a puppet script that illustrates how people influence each other in mood or self-concept. Be as comical or serious as you like. Use the outline provided below. You may wish to obtain puppets in order to enact your story on stage. On with the show!

Title:

Characters:

Setting:

Plot:

◇ Unit 6
Growing as a Person

GIVERS AND TAKERS

Directions: Read the following information about Andrew Carnegie. Then answer the questions that follow as you explore your thoughts about giving.

It has been said that "it is better to give than to receive." One of the richest men who ever lived was Andrew Carnegie. Born the son of a Scottish weaver, Andrew grew up in a very poor family. Through hard work and sound investments, he became a multimillionaire. Carnegie once said that a man who dies rich is disgraced. When he died, Carnegie left $22 million to his family. The remaining $400 million went to a worker's pension fund, public libraries, universities, and the promotion of world peace. Carnegie's actions showed that he believed in giving.

1. What is a "philanthropist"? Was Carnegie a philanthropist? _____

   _____

   _____

2. What do you think people gain from giving? _____

   _____

3. Must a person have plenty of money to be a giver? Explain your answer. _____

   _____

   _____

4. Some people can give freely but are uncomfortable with taking. Why do you think they are like this?

   _____

   _____

5. Do you think society has more givers or more takers? How is society affected by the ratio of givers to takers?

   _____

6. Explain whether you are a giver or a taker. In what ways, if any, would you like to change? How might you go about doing so?

   _____

   _____

◇ Unit 6
◇ Growing as a Person

A PERSON OF VISION

Directions: Clara Barton grew from a shy, unassuming girl into an adult of vision, determination, and courage. While she is best known for founding the American Red Cross, Barton applied her vision to many other worthwhile goals as well. Read the following passage from Leni Hamilton's biography of Clara Barton for a closer look at Barton's personality and her achievements (*Clara Barton* by Leni Hamilton, Chelsea House Publishers, New York, New Haven, Philadelphia, 1988). Then answer the questions that follow.

By nature Barton was sensitive and shy. She preferred to avoid arguments whenever she could. Yet her friend Julian Hubbell once noted that, when pressed on any subject, she could say more on the point than almost anyone. Blessed with a keen, scholarly mind, she was also very independent. For the most part, she did not enjoy working with established groups, such as the U.S. Sanitary Commission. Her preference was to strike out on her own.

A tremendous humanitarian, who was always conscious of propriety, she nevertheless defied the usual way of doing things when it presented obstacles rather than solutions. Hubbell said of her that she not only sympathized with suffering, she herself suffered. Sensitive to criticism, and often doubtful of her own self-worth, she was able to overcome the melancholy streak in her nature when she was bringing comfort to others. At such times the normally shy and ladylike ex-schoolteacher could run through a hail of bullets to do her job. She brought to her work not only a rare gift for organization but a persistence and determination that could overcome any obstacle in her path.

The life of a person with vision is often one of a struggle, of constantly fighting the status quo. Barton's life was filled with her battles for progress. She was one of the first to see the need in Bordentown for free public school education, to demonstrate that women could work alongside men in a government office, to realize that nursing must be done at the battlefront and that female nurses could be employed to do it, to create an agency to locate missing soldiers. She was among the first in her country to comprehend the importance of having the Red Cross in the United States, and she worked to make her countrymen understand this. She may have been the first person to realize that the International Red Cross could be used to aid people in times of peace. Following her lead, the United States started to help other nations with foreign aid. Whenever there was an obstacle to success, Barton overcame it.

Barton is largely remembered today for having founded the American Red Cross. Yet her accomplishments have served much more than just one country. In making sure that all victims of wars and natural disasters will be aided by trained volunteers, she became in fact a truly international figure.

(Continued on next page)

Analyzing the Passage

1. What personal strengths did Barton demonstrate? How did she make use of these?

_____

_____

_____

_____

_____

_____

2. What personal limitations did Barton have? Did she overcome these? If so, how?

_____

_____

_____

_____

_____

_____

3. Cite evidence that Clara Barton was a "person of vision."

_____

_____

_____

_____

_____

_____

◇ Unit 6
Growing as a Person

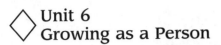
Building Academic Skills
Science

THE STRENGTH TO RESIST

Directions: Throughout time, people have struggled to deal with new scientific theories. Sometimes change has come about when young people have questioned accepted theories. They have had to prove the worth of new theories in the face of strong resistance from the establishment. One such scientist was the young Greek Hippocrates. Read the following passage about his work from the book *Scientists Who Changed the World* by Lynn and Gray Poole (Dodd, Mead & Company, New York, 1960). Then discuss the questions that follow with your class.

It seems incredible that in the same country where active bodies were so perfectly trained and conditioned, sick people received very inferior treatment. The Greek man or woman who became ill sent for a priest-physician from one of the temples. The priests had little knowledge of disease, so they practiced a primitive kind of mumbo jumbo. Some patients recovered in spite of the lack of proper care. Ignorant treatment caused the untimely death of many patients, others unnecessarily became chronic invalids.

Priest and patient accepted without question that illness itself was caused by some offense to one of the many Greek gods. The god had cast an evil spell on the offender, who became sick. Everyone believed that an evil spell was the cause of disease and that cure could be effected only by making a sacrifice to the angry god. Sometimes food and flowers were placed on the altar of the god. Frequently a pig or a sheep was sacrificed in a temple. Often the priest would examine the insides of the slaughtered beast and would find in the gory entrails an omen, good or bad, for the sick person.

After the sacrifice had been made, the priest-physician would mix herbs for the patient to take. He gave other treatments: placed charms on the body of a sick person; rattled amulets over the sickbed; or intoned incantations designed to placate the angry god. A few priest-doctors even consulted the stars to try to find out the will of the god.

The repeated rites were primitive but priest-physicians did learn from experience that certain herbs and drugs helped patients. All secrets of care and cure were jealously guarded, however, because the temple-doctors wanted to hold on to the profitable business of treating the sick. With such tight control in the hands of a very few men, it is hardly surprising that progress was slow in the priestly practice of medicine.

Revolt against soothsayers and temple-doctors started in a modest way on the Greek island of Cos off the coast of Asia Minor in the fifth century, B.C. The successful change in medical thinking and patient care, which showed the way right to the doors of our twentieth-century medical schools and hospitals, was led by a man called Hippocrates.

A native of Cos, Hippocrates went to train as a priest-physician at his island's Temple of Aesculapius, the mythological god supposed to have been the world's first doctor. The priest-physicians of the Temple accepted Hippocrates for training in the rituals of healing people made sick by angry gods.

In a very short time, Hippocrates discovered that other young men in training shared his dissatisfaction with existing methods for curing patients. The group met in secret and

(Continued on next page)

Hippocrates, its leader, said that he was sure that illness came from earthly causes. The trainees, working on the side of Hippocrates, proceeded cautiously because the established temple-doctors were too powerful to defy openly in the beginning.

Hippocrates and his friends quietly treated patients who came to the Temple of Aesculapius. Under the new leadership, a theory of medical practice evolved and gained favor on Cos. By the time the ruling class of temple-doctors realized what the young physicians were doing, the fame of Hippocrates and his colleagues had spread. Medical progress could not be stopped completely but the soothsaying physicians bitterly resisted it.

The methods that Hippocrates put into practice 2,300 years ago were the first to separate medicine from superstition, the first to give a scientific approach to medicine.

Hippocrates based his work and teaching on the firm beliefs that disease was caused by "some earthly force entering the body," or by a "breakdown of the internal organs of the body." He was convinced, too, that a doctor had to find out what caused illness before a patient could be treated.

His theories and ideas seem today to be so obvious and naïve that the simple statement of them may make us smile. But in his day the ideas were astounding and subversive. Older physicians warned that the gods would certainly punish both the believers and their patients. But the group of young medical pioneers continued to work successfully with an ever-increasing number of patients.

Gradually a new school of medical thought was established and expanded. Hippocrates developed and taught methods of patient-study and care that must have seemed strange to people who previously had been treated with chanting and strange potions. In the new system the doctor found out as much as possible about the physical state of the patient when he was well. Conditions of the skin, eyes, and even fingernails were checked. The doctor felt the patient's heartbeat and with ear to patient's chest listened to internal sounds.

The physical examination included questions similar to those asked by doctors today. The patient was asked about his symptoms, his feelings at the beginning of the illness and as it progressed. He was questioned about the normal diet of food and drink and about what he had eaten, what liquid he had swallowed just before he was taken sick.

In short, Hippocrates instructed his followers to take complete histories on patients, and to note down every fact as they progressed toward the diagnosis of illness.

For Discussion

1. What were the accepted views on illness in early Greece?

2. What "new" approaches to patient care were promoted by Hippocrates?

3. How do people respond to those who have new and different ideas?

4. What qualities in a person allow him or her to stand by convictions?

5. How can you evaluate the ideas of those people who think differently from the rest?

◇ Unit 6
◇ Growing as a Person

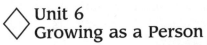

Building Academic Skills
Health

AN OATH FOR WORKING

Being a mature person means having goals to work for and rules to live by. A clear set of rules can serve as a guide for making decisions. It can help you say and do the right thing at difficult moments.

A person who enters the medical profession declares his or her dedication to the work of healing by taking the Hippocratic Oath. This oath was written in the fifth century, B.C., by the Greek physician Hippocrates. An updated version was adopted by the World Medical Association in 1948. It reads:

> *I solemnly pledge myself to consecrate my life to the service of humanity. I will give to my teachers the respect and gratitude which is their due; I will practice my profession with conscience and dignity; the health of my patient will be my first consideration; I will respect the secrets which are confided in me; I will maintain by all means in my power the honor and the noble traditions of the medical profession; my colleagues will be my brothers; I will not permit considerations of religion, nationality, race, party politics, or social standing to intervene between my duty and my patient; I will maintain the utmost respect for human life, from the time of conception; even under threat, I will not use my medical knowledge contrary to the laws of humanity. I make these promises solemnly, freely, and upon my honor.*

Directions: Think about the life's work that you would most like to pursue. Using the Hippocratic Oath as an example, write an oath for working in that field. If you are undecided about a career, write an oath that applies to your part-time job, if you have one, or to your work as a student.

Name _____ Date _____ Class Period _____

◇ Unit 6
◇ Growing as a Person

WHAT SHAPE FITS YOU?

A long time ago you learned to identify basic geometric shapes. In later math classes, you learned the specific characteristics that distinguish one shape from another.

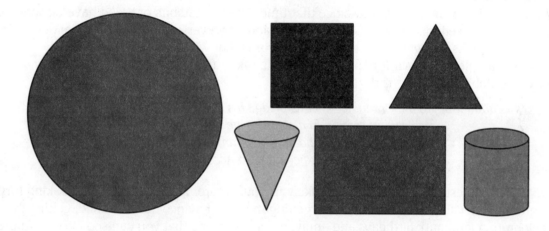

Directions: Think about the qualities of each shape above. Now relate them to your personality. Are you most like a circle? A square? Draw the shape of your choice in the box at the left. Then on the right explain your choice, relating your personality to that shape. Be sure to include specific examples to explain how your personality matches the shape you have chosen.

Shape	Comparison

◇ Unit 7
Moving Toward Independence

Building Academic Skills
Language Arts

A Toast for Every Occasion

The custom of toasting dates back to early Rome. The Roman Senate decreed that all who dined must raise their glasses in a toast to the health of the emperor Augustus. Small pieces of toasted bread were included in the custom.

Toasting practices have changed greatly since that time. The toasted bits of bread have disappeared. The carefully chosen words used to toast a person or an occasion, however, remain. The custom of toasting gives the opportunity to express thoughts and sentiments in words that will be remembered.

Here are two examples of toasts for special occasions taken from Paul Kearney's *Toasts and Anecdotes* (Grosset & Dunlap Publishers, New York, 1923).

> *Graduation:* *To the Graduate — let us pledge his health with the hope that he will always remain in a class by himself.*
>
> *Birthday:* *A toast, on your birthday, from Immaturity to Experience; from Youth to Age; from Expectation to Accomplishment.*

Directions: Several milestone experiences are likely in your future. No doubt, you are looking forward to high school graduation. Other milestones may be getting married, having your first child, getting the job you want, and celebrating landmark birthdays and anniversaries. Imagine that you can see into the future to the following moments. Write a toast for each occasion. Toasts should be about you and should reflect what you would like others to be able to say about you at that moment in time.

A Graduation Toast
A Wedding Toast
A Twenty-Fifth Anniversary Toast
A Fiftieth Birthday Toast

◇ **Unit 7**
Moving Toward Independence

Building Academic Skills
Social Studies

POOR RICHARD'S ADVICE

Directions: Ben Franklin published the first issue of *Poor Richard's Almanac* in the fall of 1732. His almanac contained clever sayings and sage advice for everyday living. Review the following selections from the almanac. (These sayings and information about Franklin's life can be found in the book *The Life and Letters of Benjamin Franklin,* E.M. Hale & Company, Eau Claire, Wisconsin.) Beside each saying, write "A" if you agree that the advice holds true today. Write "D" if you feel it does not hold true today. Be prepared to explain your responses.

_____ 1. "No man e'er was glorious, who was not laborious."

_____ 2. "He that cannot obey, cannot command."

_____ 3. "An egg to-day is better than a hen to-morrow."

_____ 4. "Keep thy shop, and thy shop will keep thee."

_____ 5. "Early to bed and early to rise, makes a man healthy, wealthy, and wise."

_____ 6. "At the working man's house hunger looks in, but dares not to enter."

_____ 7. "Lend money to an enemy, and thou'lt gain him; to a friend, and thou'lt lose him."

_____ 8. "Be always ashamed to catch thyself idle."

_____ 9. "The second Vice is Lying, the first is running in Debt."

_____ 10. "Pay what you owe, and what you're worth you'll know."

_____ 11. "Hide not your Talents, they for Use were made. What's a Sun-Dial in the Shade?"

_____ 12. "Tim was so learned, that he could name a Horse in nine languages. So ignorant, that he bought a Cow to ride."

_____ 13. "Haste makes Waste."

_____ 14. "A Child thinks 20 Shillings and 20 Years can scarce ever be spent."

_____ 15. "Laziness travels so slowly that Poverty soon overtakes him."

Building Academic Skills
Science

THE MOTHER OF INVENTION

Directions: There is an old familiar saying, "Necessity is the mother of invention." Do you believe this is true? Does needing something lead to creating something? One way to investigate the truth of the statement is to research the lives of inventors. A good example is George Eastman, who invented the Kodak camera. Read the following information about Eastman, summarized from the book *Click! A Story About George Eastman* by Barbara Mitchell (Carolrhoda Books, Inc., Minneapolis, 1986). Then discuss with your class the questions that follow.

As a boy in the 1850s and 1860s, George experienced quite a lot of necessity. After his father died, his mother ran a boarding house to try to support the family. George had two sisters, one of whom had been crippled by polio. Providing for her children became quite a struggle for the young widow Eastman, and George looked for ways to help out from a very young age. At the age of nine, he made a puzzle from his mother's old knitting needles, which he sold to another boy for ten cents. He gave the dime to his mother.

At thirteen, George took a job as a messenger. At fourteen, he became an office boy. All of George's employers noticed that he was extremely well-organized in everything he did.

George still liked to do things for his mother. One day he had a photograph of himself made for her. George became fascinated by the photography process. As a junior bookkeeper for a bank in his early twenties, George decided to purchase a camera to take on a trip to Central America. He was dismayed to find his equipment weighed almost fifty pounds! His "camera" included bottles of chemicals, a box of glass plates, and a dark tent. Carrying such equipment made travel difficult.

Several trips later, George concluded that there should be a way to make a smaller camera that would be convenient for carrying. George set out to find a solution. After a long series of experiments, George produced his first little camera in 1888. This camera weighed only twenty-two ounces and was easily held in one hand. What a great invention! George's first Kodak was the ancestor of the pocket instamatic of the twentieth century.

For Discussion

1. What forms of necessity did George experience as a boy? As a young man?

2. Do you think that George's family background could have influenced the type of person he became? If so, how?

3. Describe an instance from your own experience when someone used his or her resourcefulness to meet a need that otherwise would have gone unfulfilled.

FAMILIES TODAY Building Academic Skills

Name _____ Date _____ Class Period _____

◇ Unit 7
◇ Moving Toward Independence

Directions: Healthful habits bring many rewards to individuals and families. These include physical, mental, emotional, and social rewards. Use the space below to list several rewards under each healthful habit.

Good Eating Habits	Adequate Rest	Exercise

No Tobacco	No Alcohol	No Other Harmful Drugs

◇ Unit 7
◇ Moving Toward Independence

FAVORITE BRANDS

Consumers face hundreds of decisions in the marketplace each time they shop. Selecting the brand of product to buy is one such decision. Knowing what brands others choose may be of interest to you as a consumer. Advertisers and producers rely on data from market research. Information on product sales and consumer preferences helps them make sound business decisions. One tool for market research is the survey.

Directions: Use the survey form below. Write in a type of product and four well-known brand names of the product. Survey twenty people — at different stores, if possible — about which brand is their favorite. Use your results to determine the percentage of people surveyed who chose each brand.

PRODUCT SURVEY					
Type of Product:					
Person Surveyed	**Brand #1:**	**Brand #2:**	**Brand #3:**	**Brand #4:**	**(Other Brands)**
1.					
2.					
3.					
4.					
5.					
6.					
7.					
8.					
9.					
10.					
11.					
12.					
13.					
14.					
15.					
16.					
17.					
18.					
19.					
20.					
Percentage					

Name _____ Date _____ Class Period _____

BEDTIME

Directions: Being a skillful parent calls for strategies to handle the routines of daily living, including bedtime. Read the following passage from *Please Don't Eat the Daisies* by Jean Kerr (Doubleday & Company, Inc., Garden City, N.Y., 1957). Then discuss with your class the questions that follow.

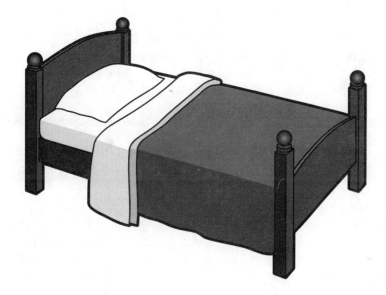

Getting a child to bed is a different proposition altogether. First you locate your child and make a simple announcement to the effect that it is now bedtime. This leads to a spirited debate in which you have to listen to a passionate defense of the many mothers of character and vision who just live up the block and who always allow their seven-year-old boys to stay up and watch Bilko. (Indeed, if my informant is correct, ours are the only children in Larchmont who don't habitually sit up to catch Night Beat.)

You gently and gracefully present your side of the picture. "Listen," you say, "I don't want to hear one more word about Rory Killilea's mother. You're going to bed right now, do you hear, now, this minute!" These persuasive remarks, declaimed in clear ringing tones with perhaps an additional "this Minute!" thrown in for good measure, are usually sufficient to get a boy up into the bedroom. Theoretically, the matter is closed. Actually, you've just begun to fight.

Now begins a series of protracted farewell appearances. He comes back on the landing to say that his pajamas are wet and he has a neat idea: he's going to sleep in his snow pants. You say it's impossible, how could those pajamas be wet? And he says he doesn't know unless it's because he used them to mop up the floor when he tipped over the fish tank.

(Continued on next page)

It shouldn't take you more than fifteen minutes to find his other pajamas — the ones that haven't got any buttons, the ones that are supposed to be in the clean-clothes hamper but aren't. When you've finally got him pinned into that dry pair, you can go back and glare at your husband, who has found the whole incident rather amusing (well, . . . he's a boy). Your husband's hilarity, however, will be somewhat quenched in a moment when he hears that one of the fish has perished in the disaster and will require an immediate burial outside by flashlight.

But soft! That boy is back again, and we are into the following dialog:

"I suppose you want me to brush my teeth."

"Of course I want you to brush your teeth."

"Okay, but I won't be going to school tomorrow."

"Why not, for heaven's sake?"

"Because I'll be poisoned to death."

"What are you talking about?"

"Chris used my toothbrush to paint his model car."

This necessitates a brief but painful interview with Chris, who declares, "He never used that toothbrush anyway; he always used mine."

Normally, along about here, you can count on a seven-minute Luftpause during which you can cut out a recipe for Baked Alaska which you will make as soon as you lose ten pounds, which will be never.

But we're ready for that third appearance. "Mommy" — this time the voice is dripping with tragedy — "Mommy, it's raining."

You leap out of your chair.

"Do you mean to tell me that you got up just to tell me it's raining? I know it's raining. Go back to bed!"

He goes back, but presently the sound of muffled sobs come flooding down the stairwell. Naturally, you have to go upstairs and turn on the light and find out what's the matter with the poor thing. What's the matter, it turns out, is that he has left his bicycle over on the Slezaks' lawn. Not that he is at all concerned about the bicycle, which he has just got for Christmas and which cost thirty-nine dollars and ninety-five cents, but he has tied a keen foxtail to the handle bar and it will be ruined, just absolutely ruined. So you can go over and get the bicycle and if you hurry you'll be back in time to catch his fourth and final appearance.

This time, noticing the edge of hysteria in your voice (he's been around for seven years; he knows when you are going to crack), he keeps his message brief.

"Mommy, this is important. I have to have a costume for the play tomorrow. I'm Saint Joseph."

For Discussion

1. What tactics did the child in this passage use to delay bedtime?

2. Sometimes exaggeration adds to the humor of a story situation while still pointing out the reality. Is this true in this selection? Explain your answer.

3. This book was written in the 1950s. Do you think the same scene might be different in any ways today? Explain your answer.

4. Why do you think children sometimes resist going to bed?

5. For each reason you listed in the previous question, identify one positive way caregivers could respond to it.

● ◇ Unit 8
Forming Your Own Family

Building Academic Skills
Social Studies

FIRST LADIES

A study of America's "first families" reflects changing roles of wives and husbands over the past 200 years. The book *Our First Ladies,* by Jane and Burt McConnnell (Thomas Y. Crowell Company, New York, 1957), presents a factual account of the personal lives of many of the first ladies and their husbands, the presidents of the United States. Many types of marriage partnerships can be seen.

Directions: Read the following passages from *Our First Ladies.* As you read, think about the roles that Martha Washington and Eleanor Roosevelt had. Then discuss with your class the questions that follow.

Martha Washington (First Lady 1789–1797)

There have been many discussions as to whether the marriage of Martha and George was one of convenience, rather than true love. As the Royal Governor's most dependable officer, Washington had made a name for himself, even at twenty-seven. There was also the fact that he had declared his devotion to more than one Virginia belle; and it was well known that Martha had not lacked suitors. The real test of their romance is found in a life companionship of forty years, at home in Virginia, in military posts, in travel over dusty and muddy roads, and in the artificial social atmosphere of New York and Philadelphia. During those forty years, there were admiration, helpfulness, sincerity, fondness, and consideration on both sides. Both were swept along by events, but in their hearts they preferred the simple life of the plantation owner.

Certainly the sixteen years immediately following the marriage of Martha Custis and George Washington were happy ones. Washington had inherited Mount Vernon from his half-brother, Lawrence, who had served under Admiral Vernon and had named the estate in the Admiral's honor.

On the journey to Mount Vernon, with the Custis children, they visited Washington's sister Betty (Mrs. Fielding Lewis) at her home in Fredericksburg and made a trip across the Rappahannock so that Martha could meet Washington's mother. And they called upon other relatives and friends on the way.

Nowadays it is difficult to imagine how Martha Washington and other women of the period were able to manage their large households and entertain the relatives and friends who constantly came and went from one plantation to another. Martha's day started at sunrise. Almost always, there were guests for breakfast; and she presided graciously, making the tea and coffee herself. She thoroughly enjoyed running the establishment, and was devoted to her two children. Washington, having no youngsters of his own, lavished the affection of his generous nature upon them. In his carefully kept records we find him, year after year, sending orders to London and Paris for clothing, furniture, silks and satins, handkerchiefs, gloves, stockings, and shoes. For little Patsy there were fans, bonnets, dresses, and toys. Once the master of Mount Vernon ordered "six little books for children beginning to read, 10 shillings' worth of toys, and a box of gingerbread toys and sugar images and comfits."

●

(Continued on next page)

Eleanor Roosevelt (First Lady 1933–1945)

As First Lady of the White House, Eleanor Roosevelt led an even busier life (than she had as Governor's wife). As ears and eyes for her husband, she traveled all over the country, and often abroad, flying or driving off at a moment's notice, studying conditions, addressing Campfire Girls, Girl Scouts, and many other organizations, and returning to give careful reports to the President.

During the first year of his administration, she traveled 38,000 miles; in the second, 42,000 miles; in the third, 35,000. After that, the reporters admitted they had lost count. No woman ever took up her duties as First Lady with such a groundwork of political experience as did Eleanor Roosevelt. She worked with the women's division of the Democratic State Committee in New York for six years; she worked in political campaigns for Alfred E. Smith and for her husband. She toured the country making campaign speeches long before going to the White House. As First Lady, she broke all traditions, not only by traveling around the country on missions of interest to her husband, but by pursuing an active career of her own. Despite her mother-in-law's objections to her earning money, she made public appearances, talked over the radio, went on planned, paid lecture tours, wrote for newspapers and magazines, ran a syndicated column, "My Day," and later signed a contract for a page in a woman's magazine under the title, "If You Ask Me."

At the White House, Mrs. Roosevelt organized her household affairs so well that they needed little supervision on her part. She rode over Boulder Dam and Norris Dam in a "bucket"; she flew around the globe. Yet she still found time to have afternoon tea with her husband when she was at home, and to give him lengthy reports on what she had seen and heard in her travels.

During World War II, her interest in our fighting men led her to visit England, when she saw the work of the British women in the war and visited American troops abroad. In 1943 she made a flying trip to the Pacific, wearing the uniform of the Red Cross; in the spring of 1944 she toured the Caribbean and South American bases. Wherever she went, she talked with the men and women in our armed forces, and she brought back to her husband in Washington a clear picture of what was going on.

Because of these trips, and because in other ways she did not conform to the traditions of the other First Ladies, she became the center of a storm of criticism. Hideous caricatures of her constantly appeared in hostile newspapers, and countless jokes were made about her propensity for traveling. She herself enjoyed some of the jokes, particularly one which originated in her own family circle. One day during the war, when she was scheduled to visit a prison in Baltimore, she had to leave the White House very early in the morning, long before her husband was awake, so she did not say good-bye to him. On his way to the office later, President Roosevelt called to Miss Thompson, whom they always called "Tommy," and asked where his wife was.

"She's in prison, Mr. President!" Tommy said.

"I'm not surprised," said Franklin D. Roosevelt, "but what for?"

For Discussion

1. Describe the role of Martha Washington as wife and First Lady.
2. Describe the role of Eleanor Roosevelt as wife and First Lady.
3. Compare and contrast how these two First Ladies handled their responsibilities.
4. Were the differences between Martha and Eleanor more accountable to time period or personality? Explain your answer.
5. Are wives today more like Martha or Eleanor? Explain your answer.

Name _____ Date _____ Class Period _____

◇ Unit 8
◇ Forming Your Own Family

USING THE SCIENTIFIC METHOD

Directions: The scientific method can serve as an excellent guide for making wise decisions. Read the information that follows about the method and then try applying it to a question in your own life.

THE SCIENTIFIC METHOD

1. Define the problem or question to be answered.
2. Form a hypothesis or possible answer.
3. Experiment; collect and examine data.
4. Form a conclusion.

Forming your own family means making important decisions — whom to marry, when to marry, whether to have children, and many more. Making sound decisions is important in order to solve problems and build a strong family life. Here is an example of how Chandler used the scientific method to decide whether he was genuinely in love.

1. **Question.** Chandler asked, "Am I in love?"
2. **Hypothesis.** Chandler proposed, "I believe I am in love."
3. **Testing the Hypothesis.** Chandler used a checklist to examine his feelings.

___✓___ Feelings developed gradually and have lasted.

_____ Loved one accepted as is, with no desire to change her.

___✓___ Feelings remain when apart.

_____ Her needs come before my own.

_____ I have a happy outlook on life and zest for work.

_____ Feelings based on many traits, both desirable and less desirable.

_____ Confident about her commitment to relationship.

_____ Differences between the two of us are accepted.

___✓___ Problems are faced directly.

___✓___ Confidence in our relationship gives us both patience.

4. **Conclusion.** Because Chandler checked only four of the ten characteristics, he concluded that his feelings were not a lasting form of love.

APPLICATION

Use the scientific method to answer one of the following questions. Follow the example given. Create a checklist to use in collecting data for Step 3.

1. Am I ready for a steady relationship?
2. Am I ready for marriage?
3. Are _____ and I compatible?
4. Do I want to be a parent someday?

◇ **Unit 8**
Forming Your Own Family

FAMILY HEALTH RISKS

Directions: Read the information below. Then read the case study and discuss with your class the questions that follow.

Decisions about when or whether to have children are influenced by many factors. Family health history is often one of these.

It helps you to know what diseases, if any, run in your family and your spouse's family. Generally speaking, the odds of your children having a hereditary disease are greater when the disease has occurred in primary relatives — parents, siblings, grandparents, aunts, and uncles. Health histories of secondary relatives, such as nieces, nephews, cousins, and great-grandparents, are also helpful in recognizing patterns of disease in families. Risks are greater when more than one relative has had a hereditary disease. Other signs of hereditary influence include occurrence of disease at an early age or in spite of a healthful lifestyle.

Conditions that can increase the likelihood of a certain disease can also be inherited, such as a tendency toward high cholesterol, which may lead to a heart attack. Furthermore, research has shown some degree of genetic influence in other major diseases — diabetes, coronary heart disease, and cancer. Heredity can make one more susceptible to allergies, asthma, migraine headaches, obesity, osteoporosis, rheumatoid arthritis, miscarriages, stillbirths, and birth defects.

CASE STUDY

James and Gina are an engaged couple who are making a decision about whether to have children. They are concerned about the health of any children they decide to have. Gina, her father, and her brother all have asthma and various allergies to airborne substances. James, too, has mild asthma and a few allergies. Both Gina and James have their asthma conditions under control, although Gina has been hospitalized several times over the years during asthma attacks.

For Discussion

1. What do you think concerns Gina and Jim?

2. What problems might Gina and Jim face should they decide to have children?

3. How important is the risk of passing on diseases to children when making the decision to have children?

4. How would you advise Jim and Gina?

FAMILIES TODAY Building Academic Skills
Copyright © Glencoe/McGraw-Hill

◇ **Unit 8**
Forming Your Own Family

FOR RICHER OR POORER

In most wedding ceremonies, couples pledge their love and loyalty to each other through all conditions and circumstances, including "for richer or poorer." Sadly, when problems arise, vows are all too often forgotten. It has been said that "love goes out the window when hard times come knocking on the door."

Developing a family budget can help couples avoid difficult financial times and stay together when they do occur. Couples who have compromised and agreed on expenses have shown the teamwork needed for a successful marriage.

Directions: Pair up with a classmate to complete the budget below. Begin by selecting your combined income level. Then decide on the number of children in the family. Next, determine your monthly expenses for each category listed. Use your own knowledge or do some brief research. Be sure to add in all expenses that would be included in each category. Adjust amounts, as needed, to be sure that total expenditures do not exceed total income.

OUR FAMILY BUDGET

Net Monthly Income (select one):

_____ $1,440 with full family health coverage

_____ $2,500 with limited family health coverage

_____ $3,450 with employee health coverage only

_____ $2,900 with no insurance plan

_____ $ _____ (other approved by teacher)

Number of children:

_____ None   _____ 3

_____ 1   _____ 4

_____ 2   _____ 5 or more

Monthly Expenses	Monthly Amount
Rent	$
Utilities	$
Food	$
Transportation	$
Child Care	$
Clothing	$
Insurance	$
Entertainment	$
Savings	$
Miscellaneous	$
Total	$

◆◆◆◆Building Academic Skills Answer Key◆◆◆◆

Unit 1: The Family Foundation

Fran Tarkenton: A Look at Values

1. Possible answers may include: **determination,** shown by setting goals and working to achieve them as well as playing football despite asthma; **positive attitude,** shown by saying "We'll whip 'em next time" after a big loss; **love of sports,** shown by playing three sports; and **academic achievement,** shown by being a good student.
2. Fran was raised in a family with a religious framework that probably influenced his values in many positive ways. A minister, his father saw Fran's interest and ability in sports as an inspiration from God.

Democracy and Family

1. Like a family, democracy binds people, as in a brotherhood.
2. One half is individualism, which isolates people. The other half brings people together, making all races like comrades. Yes, because people in a family need to learn to be individuals who can act and think independently, but they also need the support and sustenance provided within a family unit.
3. Selected definitions will vary depending on dictionary used and definitions chosen. Students may note that they are similar in that both families and people in a democracy work together for the good of all. Also, they are both made up of a group of people who have some common link, and they both ideally make decisions via those in charge, with input from all. They differ in the way they are formed, in size, in purpose, and in many details of operating.

What's New?

Answers will vary but may include the following:

Air conditioning — made city life more bearable in the summer; contributed to rising population in the Sun Belt. **Computer** — allowed for rapid exchange of huge amounts of information. **Fax machine** — provided a way for people to transmit documents without the need for physically carrying them or mailing them. **Polio vaccine** — families relieved of worry that their children would be killed or disabled by this dreadful disease. **Teflon** — made low-fat cooking easier, contributing to people's health. **Television** — became a substitute for family games.

Students' descriptions of changes the twenty-first century may bring will vary.

A Long and Happy Life

Answers will vary, but students may note that longer lives will mean more years during middle-age, giving people more time and opportunity for additional careers, recreation after children are grown, and enjoyment of grandchildren. On the other hand, illnesses may reduce the quality of life in the later years.

Slice the Family Pie

Results will vary. Some students may need help in converting percentages to degrees. They should multiply the percent figure by 3.6. (Example: For 45%, multiply 45 by 3.6 to get 162 degrees.)

Unit 2: Strengthening Relationships

The True Story

Answers will vary.

A House Divided

Compositions will vary.

Relationships

Answers will vary but may include the idea that humans depend on one another, indicating a symbiotic relationship. For example, an infant needs parental care to survive. Human relationships also show competitiveness. When there are conflicting needs in a family, someone's priorities must usually change so that family members can continue to coexist. For example, an older child in a family might have to give up some time with friends to take care of a younger sister while the parent is working.

Family Wellness

Answers will vary.

Family Vacations

Answers will vary.

♦ ♦ ♦ ♦ ♦

Unit 3: Managing with Insight

Is It Really *Cheaper by the Dozen?*

1. "Motion economy" is using the quickest and most effortless way to get a job done. Examples may include taking moving pictures of children washing dishes and buttoning vest from bottom up.
2. Answers will vary.
3. Management charts used to show when jobs get done. In the morning Dad included tooth brushing, bath taking, hair combing, and bed making. At night he included weighing, homework, washing hands and face, and tooth brushing.
4. Answers will vary.
5. He helped them learn organization, attention to detail, and efficiency.
6. Answers will vary.
7. He discovered that he lost time in the end when he had to deal with cutting himself.
8. He joked about disciplining the neighbor child, thinking he was one of theirs.
9. Answers will vary, but students should note that a sense of humor can contribute to a happy environment and help people get through difficult moments.
10. Answers will vary.

His and Her Expectations

Answers will vary.

The Other Half of the Story

1. **Packaging is bad** — when food is packaged, manufacturers are likely to find uses for the waste; packaging reduces spoilage.

   Recycling is always good — curbside garbage-recycling programs often require more fuel consumption due to additional collection trucks, creating more pollution; more paper recycling means fewer trees are planted for commercial harvesting.

   Nonbiodegradable products are bad — most modern landfills inhibit biodegradation of anything due to capping; biodegradable products can leach dangerous chemicals into water supplies.

   Disposables are bad — even though juice boxes create waste, transporting empty bottles takes fuel, contributing to air pollution; cloth diapers use water for cleaning, while disposables do not.

   Plastics are bad — plastics take less energy to manufacture than aluminum and glass.
2. Probably more reliable if done by an independent research organization because it might not have an interest in promoting the use of packaging. People should always look at who generates studies and who supports those studies financially.
3. Environmental issues are clearly not easy to settle. As this article points out, what may seem like a solution can create other problems that may even be of equal or greater concern.
4. No. It simply reinforces that careful appraisals of consequences are necessary whenever solutions are sought.

The Best of Care

Allergist — allergies to foods and substances; **audiologist** — hearing problems; **cardiologist** — heart; **dental hygienist** — tooth cleaning; **dentist** — tooth problems; **dermatologist** — skin; **emergency medical technician** — first aid and other initial care for victims of accidents or serious illness; **gastroenterologist** — stomach; **geriatric physician** — elderly; **gynecologist** — health problems of females; **neurologist** — nervous system; **obstetrician** — pregnancy and delivery; **oncologist** — cancer; **ophthalmologist** — eyes; **orthopedist** — skeletal disorders; **pediatrician** — children; **pharmacist** — prescription drugs; **physical therapist** — rehabilitation; **podiatrist** — feet; **psychiatrist** — mental illness (can prescribe medication); **psychologist** — mind and behavior (cannot prescribe medication); **respiratory therapist** — lungs; **urologist** — urinary tract.

Out to Eat?

Answers will vary.

♦ ♦ ♦ ♦ ♦

Unit 4: Supporting Family and Friends

The Painful Side of Divorce

1. Possible answers are: Chris is shocked and angry. He vents his frustration and takes his anger out in ways that are not harmful. Jenny is young and may not understand what is going on. She knows something is wrong, because she curls in a ball seeking comfort. She also turns to Bunny for comfort. Mom seems sad and thoughtful as she stares down at the table. She may be suffering and insecure about what to do, because she offers no comments about

the situation. Dad is painfully matter-of-fact about the situation. Although he may be trying to show strength, his approach seems to lack sensitivity and his manner indicates that he is doing something uncomfortable that he just wants to be done with.

2. Living apart from family members; changes in routine; new surroundings; managing relationships differently.

3. The Halloween pumpkins symbolized family. They were falling apart, just as the family was. Angry at the idea of a broken home, Chris takes physical action against that idea by exploding the pumpkins.

4. Answers will vary. Encourage students to see that although this attitude may feel true at times, people can do much to prevent problems and to recover from them.

Leaders
Answers will vary.

Freud — After a Loved One Dies
1. **Shock and numbness** shown by an inability to work and wandering restlessly; **reality** shown by the stress and depressed feelings he had and the physical ailments that are symptoms of grief.
2. Attended to practical details that would give comfort.
3. Because of the pressures he felt from challenges to his theories, his strong reaction to his father's death, and his conflict with Fliess.
4. Yes. It may take as much as two years to work through the grief process after the death of a parent.

No Easy Answer
Possible reasons for prolonging life — younger age of person; chance for recovery exists; strong feelings of people involved. **Possible reasons for allowing natural death** — existence of living will; wishes of family; no hope for recovery; pain and suffering of individual; older age of individual; religious convictions; expense of medical technology.

Answers will vary but may include person who's dying (if her or she has made a living will) and close family members. Students should support their answers.

Drugs and Crime
1. 21.2 percent
2. Robbery
3. Rape

4. 1.8 percent
5. 36.2 percent
6. 23.5 percent
7. 40.4 percent
8. 100.1 percent; no, chart explains that rounding can cause this

◆ ◆ ◆ ◆ ◆ ◆
Unit 5: Extending Your Relationships

Speaking of Seniors
Questions will vary but may include those about seniors' lives as teenagers, memorable events in the history of the world and community, and lifestyles of the past.

A Personal Bill of Rights
Answers will vary but may include: the right to be free from physical or emotional abuse; the right to express oneself without fear of ridicule; and the right to maintain a degree of personal independence within a relationship.

Magnetic Personalities
1. Possibly both, since characteristics of personality can be both inherited and developed.
2. Opposites may attract initially, but unless those involved are compatible in some areas, particularly in their values and beliefs, the relationship will probably not last long.
3. Yes. They may come by it naturally or have worked to make themselves appealing to others. Some have better examples to follow than others do.
4. Possible answers are: extrovertedness; concern for others; sense of humor; sincerity; high self-worth.

Prescription for Elders
Answers will vary.

Dates and Dollars
Answers will vary.

◆ ◆ ◆ ◆ ◆ ◆
Unit 6: Growing as a Person

Pulling Strings
Answers will vary.

Givers and Takers
1. Someone who takes an active effort to promote good will and human welfare. Yes.
2. Good feelings from helping others; elevated self-worth; pride; reciprocal actions.

3. No. People who have less can give less. They can also give time and energy in different ways, as through volunteer efforts.
4. May have low self-worth, feeling they are not worthy of receiving; may feel that they always have to win approval by giving to others.
5. Answers will vary according to optimistic/ pessimistic points of view and student experiences. Too many takers in society can contribute to society's weakness.
6. Answers will vary.

A Person of Vision
Answers will vary but may include:
1. Barton demonstrated intelligence, independence, compassion, organization, and determination. She used these to accomplish the numerous feats cited in the passage.
2. Barton was shy, sensitive to criticism, sometimes self-doubting. She overcame these limitations by focusing on helping others and achieving her goals.
3. Barton founded the American Red Cross. She also worked to expand the role of the International Red Cross; to secure public education; to advance women's employment opportunities; to improve battlefield nursing practices; and to find missing soldiers.

The Strength to Resist
1. Illness was caused by offending the gods; a priest-physician had to be consulted to learn how to placate the gods and cure the illness.
2. Hippocrates believed that illness had earthly causes and cures. Physicians could learn these by examining a patient's physical condition and asking questions about the patient's behavior prior to becoming ill.
3. Often with fear, ridicule, or lack of understanding.
4. High self-esteem; assertiveness; self-confidence; faith in knowledge and ability; perseverance.
5. Examine their credibility by looking at their experience, level of knowledge, reliability, and resources.

An Oath for Working
Answers will vary.

What Shape Fits You?
Answers will vary.

◆ ◆ ◆ ◆ ◆ ◆
Unit 7: Moving Toward Independence

A Toast for Every Occasion
Answers will vary.

Poor Richard's Advice
Answers will vary.

The Mother of Invention
Answers will vary but may include:
1. As a boy, needed money; needed to help mother and sisters. As a young man, needed convenient camera.
2. Poverty taught him value of hard work, thrift, resourcefulness; closeness to family and sister's polio developed desire to make life easier, more convenient for people.
3. Answers will vary.

Rewards Offered!
Answers will vary but may include:
Good Eating Habits — physical strength; improved ability to fight disease, deal with stress; improved appearance.
Adequate Rest — better performance at school and work; improved appearance; improved resistance to disease.
Exercise — improved physical and mental health; improved appearance; opportunities for socializing.
No Tobacco — better physical health; avoiding addiction; avoiding disease; more social acceptability; financial savings.
No Alcohol — better physical and mental health; avoiding addiction; avoiding legal troubles; avoiding dangerous situations; financial savings.
No Other Harmful Drugs — avoiding serious mental and physical problems; avoiding addiction; avoiding legal troubles; avoiding causing pain to friends and family.

Favorite Brands
Results will vary.

◆ ◆ ◆ ◆ ◆ ◆
Unit 8: Forming Your Own Family

Bedtime
1. He claimed friends' parents allowed them to stay up late; needed dry pajamas; had problem with toothbrush; wanted to bury fish; left bike out in rain; needed costume.
2. Probably yes. Although children do stretch the issue at bedtime, all of what happened might be unusual for one night. Put together, however, it adds to the humor, since the frustration is typical for parents who deal with these kinds

is typical for parents who deal with these kinds of circumstances regularly.

3. In many homes, it would. Here the mother appears to be totally responsible for dealing with the boy. Nowadays, fathers are likely to be involved too.

4. They may have trouble settling down, be afraid, be involved in enjoyable activity, want to feel adult, or have formed a habit of seeking attention this way.

5. To help a child settle down, they might read a story or have some quiet activity before bedtime. To help an insecure child, they might provide a night light, leave the door slightly open, supply a cuddly toy, and always give the child love and reassurance. When the child doesn't want to leave a pleasant activity, caregivers can remind the child that the activity can be continued the next day. To help the child feel adult, they can communicate in an adult way and reinforce that adults need their sleep, too. To break a bad habit, they can be firm and consistent about bedtime.

First Ladies

1. Martha was a companion to her husband, the manager of household, a hostess to guests, and a mother.

2. Eleanor was a companion to her husband, an organized household manager, an information gatherer for her husband, and a campaigner, political activist, lecturer, and writer.

3. Martha spent much time and energy with household duties, including hostessing, while Eleanor organized the home front so that she didn't have to be there, freeing her to tackle all sorts of issues and situations that were not usually female territory in those and earlier times. Eleanor was less conventional than Martha, leaving herself open to criticism.

4. Probably both. Although Eleanor broke traditions, she probably couldn't have done as much in earlier eras. Her strength, intelligence, conviction, and fortitude allowed her to be different at a time when it was possible although not always accepted.

5. Some wives enjoy staying on the home front as Martha did. Many, however, combine home responsibilities with careers and political interests.

Using the Scientific Method
Answers will vary.

Family Health Risks

1. Any children they have are likely to have allergy/asthma problems, since both parents have histories of such difficulties. They may worry that the children could be especially hard hit because of inheritance from both parents.

2. Dealing with ill children; hospital and other medical expenses; stress.

3. Answers will vary. Students may note that the seriousness of the affliction and the degree of possibility of inheritance may have an effect on the decision.

4. Communicate with each other and experts (physicians). Examine their own feelings. If desired, explore other parenting possibilities. Recognize that risks accompany any birth.

For Richer or Poorer
Answers will vary.